Poet of Death

Kirk C. Olson

POET OF DEATH

iUniverse books may be ordered through booksellers or by contacting:

iUniverse
1663 Liberty Drive
Bloomington, IN 47403
www.iuniverse.com
844-349-9409

Because of the dynamic nature of the Internet, any web addresses or links contained in this book may have changed since publication and may no longer be valid. The views expressed in this work are solely those of the author and do not necessarily reflect the views of the publisher, and the publisher hereby disclaims any responsibility for them.

Any people depicted in stock imagery provided by Getty Images are models, and such images are being used for illustrative purposes only.
Certain stock imagery © Getty Images.

ISBN: 978-1-6632-2966-3 (sc)
ISBN: 978-1-6632-2967-0 (e)

Library of Congress Control Number: 2021919808

Print information available on the last page.

iUniverse rev. date: 10/20/2021

Dedication

To the poisonous lies I loved and trusted and hoped would not exist, and the painful truth that broke my soul and my heart. I allowed them to destroy me temporarily. I am hopeful that I made a positive impact in some way that helped you.

Special Thanks

To my best friend, Rob Crapo, you kept me alive. You never judged me and were relentless with the truth that I did not want to believe. Your friendship never wavered as you patiently put back the pieces of what was left of me.

Appreciation

To Janna, Orion, Owen, Oliver

To Alison Benfeito, thank you once again for writing the foreword to this book. You are the first to read my poems/songs. I appreciate your time!

Contents

Foreword

I met Kirk Olson at my son's soccer game ten years ago. After the initial introductory phase, we soon began to converse about his passion for writing and heavy metal music. As a college graduate with a degree in English literature, I was fascinated by this "soccer dad's" organic skill for writing poetry. I hadn't yet experienced the allure of dark poetry and found it both real and addicting.

Kirk Olson's third collection of poetry is an anthology of dark fiction that explores the beauty within the very heart of darkness. Although a work of fiction, his poetry centers on realistic threats, such as domestic violence, substance abuse, madness, and death. His descriptive style and details make his poetry familiar and identifiable to the reader.

In each poem, Olson's voice reads as eerie and bone-chilling, yet at its center, it is a voice full of love and hope. Each poem maintains its intensity and brisk pace while allowing room for the reader to explore and reflect. The collection explores the delicate complexities of love-hate relationships with brutal honesty. It is deeply thoughtful and deeply emotional. It is both horrifying and brilliant.

> Conceal your boozing,
> Conceal your bruising
> Falling apart while
> Falling down.

> From "Fate of Princess Perception"
> —Alison Benfeito

Acknowledgments

Cover model: Alison Benfeito

Photographer Front Cover: Valencio Small,
Valencio/Valencio Photography
Photographer of Puppeteer Front Cover and Author
Picture Back Cover: E. K. Rogers Photography
Cothinker: R. Crapo, "Sunset Kills Us"
Photographer Sunset Back Cover: Rob Crapo

✝ Salt Fields ✝

How many acres have you given up
In your field of dreams?
None were stolen, just ignored.
Unattended to it seems.

So many things have died inside me
That were not part of a suicide.
Soul-crushing moments, choices I made
Not to swim against the tide.

Future exploded from historic pressure.
Can't stop anything blowing in the winds.
Fragments fall through my fingers,
Grasping at seeds that only root in my sins.

Tears of blood have caused a flood.
Predictions of the past are guaranteed.
All my love and lust has turned to dust
In my tumbleweed.

The boy I was, was not supposed to wade
Into this defeated dreamer of desolate lands.
Not sure what happened to his sea of dreams;
All I have is salt in my bone-dry hands.

✝ Poet of Death ✝

I just took
My last breath,
Welcomed by
The poet of death.

I just became
Oh, so frail.
Feel my finger;
It's my coffin's nail.

No sight
Or sound,
Some bodies buried
Underground.

Some cried
When I died.
Matters not
If it was suicide.

Relax, there is no pain.
There is no pleasure,
No truth. Understanding
What a worthless treasure.

All relieved, can't believe
I must sing the song.
Two religions can't be right,
Knowing now all are wrong.

No searing heat,
No chilling cold.
I was lucky;
I got to grow old.

Two die every second
While four are born.
Can't be concerned
Living objects of scorn.

No longer am I able
To see color as I dream.
Half instantly into blackness,
Souls the poet will redeem.

I die every night.
Temporarily I sleep,
Every morning alive.
Been dead so long I weep.

Life's mystery is revealed.
Poet of death lets you see
Now we are godless,
Now we are free.

Secret of death,
Alone, there is no one to tell.
No meaning of life,
No heaven and hell.

✝ Sole Believer ✝

Amen has always been an omen.
All excuses I don't condone.
Don't believe anyone.
You die and chase dreams alone.

Starting mark is lined
On a dead-end street,
Being left behind
Before you move your feet.

Before you feel uninspired,
Bank on no one is going to help.
Don't become defeated.
Beat your dreams to a pulp.

There is a moment before
Chasing the burning desire,
You believe that you will
Be showering in fire.

No consequence for being human,
Yet you say your courtesy prayers.
Deep within waiting for the end of time,
Still you believe you wasted years.

There are too many maybes
Deciding what dreams are worth.
Give birth to your babies
Even on your last day on earth.

✝ Your Dark Knight ✝

No pretension for attention.
Consuming beauty, no prevention.
Extreme efforts to gain
Some relief from the pain.

I stumble, I fall.
I was at your altar call.
My soul always free.
And you still love me.

I try, I fail.
You know from where I hail.
I run and hide.
You still are on my side.

I love, I abort.
I exist without a cohort.
A disciple of none,
Still you never would shun.

My obsessions and
My confessions
I can't sublimate.
Desire designed to emanate.

Smell of your skin
As I inhale the sin.
Holding you, my breath
Won't exhale until death.

Not a phoenix, a black swan.
All my love long gone
Can't last, a frozen rainbow
That crumbles into my shadow.

One shot, so narrow,
Nicked by Cupid's broken arrow.
Heart's hope dripped into a spill.
Love me, forever still.

Tragic the conclusion.
Magic, not illusion.
The pain only you know,
A threshold so shallow.

Last song, last dance,
For forever I would chance.
My ghost is so brave.
Dance with me upon my grave.

✝ The End ✝

I saw through God's eyes.
First he showed me earth,
Turning gray fast,
No possibility for rebirth.

Some hoped, some prayed
Damage we could reverse,
Denying and ignoring the abuse.
Then he showed me the universe

Selling improvements
Instead of sharing.
Caring about profit
Instead of caring.

All connected through
Time and space.
Yet on Mother Earth,
We continued to deface.

Deeper than what can be seen,
Destroying everything to her core.
Blasting our presence into outer space,
Claiming it is ours to explore.

Is it so hard to do,
Look, don't touch?
We have ruined,
Continued to ruin, so much.

Pray what you got to pray.
He showed me how it will end.
Neither a push of a button
Nor a click of a pen.

Nothing more to know.
Nothing else to learn.
No one there to witness.
Ball of ice in slow burn.

The beginning.

✝ Mom O. ✝

Someday turned into today,
Broken heart because she will pass.
There for my first breath,
Here for her last.

My bleeding heart
Creates a canyon of sorrow
That divides my life
Up to today and starting tomorrow.

Time to let go
And say goodbye,
Recalling memories;
She was first to see me cry.

Seventy-eight summers,
Forty-nine with me.
Within minutes,
Her soul was set free.

Lifetime of lessons
She helped me compile.
Lesson of a lifetime,
Watching her unable to smile.

Tears on my face,
Heart on my sleeve,
Holding my father and brothers,
We begin to grieve.

Counting the steps to the church,
Going over the stages of grief.
Every step forward
Stepping away from disbelief.

† Masterpiece of Delusion †

Right out of the black,
A masterpiece of delusion.
Permission to adopt my heart,
Remission to adapt my confusion.

Everything exists outside me.
Inside is desolation.
Guitar strings, my vocal chords
Screaming my postulation.

Inside, heartache is silence.
Imagination makes love boundless.
Among the corrosive carnage,
Inward hate rages soundless.

Roots are raw emotions.
No bark for first line of defense.
Buried as deep as viable
So a love affair won't commence.

Like seeds outside the strawberry,
My soul resides upon my skin.
Your tattoos are stories of love;
My scars tell tales of sin.

Brilliance is unbalanced,
Venting my superstition.
Sessions of transference
Rupturing your intuition.

✝ Dead Serious ✝

You had your moment of violence.
We had our moment of silence.

Only one war crime, that is to begin warfare,
Protecting our freedom with valor we declare.

We'll be furious in our ascent,
Vengeance for our innocent.

You left us no choice.
Our murdered you rejoice.

Superpowers were learning
As the towers were burning.

Your celebration made the world nauseate.
You won't hear us as we retaliate.

For you, nothing will ever be pristine.
It is not to be but B2 and F16.

Dead serious with words of war,
Never should have knocked on our door.

Our freedom preserved again by war.
Your life is temporary in your corridor.

You will be forgotten; dead cannot forgive.
Certain dates of history we will not relive.

You sealed your children's fate.
Only humans know hate breeds hate.

Insanity congregates all thoughtless ilk.
Nothing can exist by killing mothers' milk.

Exterminating you is freedom's conditioned response.
You'll be a temporary distraction from our renaissance.

✝ Picking Up Dreams ✝

I'm picking up broken dreams
On youth's highway of distractions.
Ripped, torn, beaten, and bruised,
Discarded among the interactions.

Dreams of the red carpet.
Onstage, singing your song.
Writing the book inside you.
In deserted ditches, dreams don't belong.

Desired dreams so important,
At one time were all held equal,
Resolved, as revolving failures.
Nightmares replaying an identical sequel.

A dream you cannot capture.
Dream catchers are another sad fable.
Consciously carry it within you,
Only way to make it inescapable.

Carried within your head to death
Creates scars that remain internal.
Carried within your heart to reality
Coordinates stars for its life eternal.

Decaying passions litter the landscape.
Someone giving up to feed the scapegoat.
The one thing that meant everything,
The dream lost, away it will float.

All dreams reside and collide here.
Breathless, without believers, they just lie
Frozen between the subconscious spectrum.
Save the dreams before they die.

Some imagined so big.
I wonder why they are here
Instead of completing,
Decided to hate their career.

A crack in another so small,
I can't believe it's here at all.
What happened to the person?
Dream remained; they went AWOL.

Everyone heard you;
You weren't alone at all.
They were on the other side
Of success and its paper-thin wall.

Who did this dream belong to?
Did it have to be put down?
This one looks very similar to many.
Was it in alcohol that it drowned?

This one seems complete; how did it end?
Life handed them something else to do?
Oh, I see the grim reaper was here,
Travelling the wrong way in lane number 2.

Bleeding slowly, some dreams
Dropped due to health.
Death of some dreamers,
Punishment for affecting another's wealth.

✝ Write Your Own Religion ✝

Write your own religion
With power and pride.
Write it while you're young,
So there is time to modify.

Bible of your beliefs,
Declaration in its rawest form.
Acknowledge what you know so far.
With experience, you will edit in your dorm.

Write your own religion.
Make it hard and cold.
The simpler you inscribe,
Ensures you'll understand it when you're old.

It only matters what you think.
You'll live it as your code.
Your set of laws to live by
Strictly detailing your mode.

Chapters of beliefs,
Be confident that you will not adjust.
If you do, just add an appendix.
It's your heart that you must trust.

Write many or just one commandment,
An effort of goodwill.
Impossible living by your decree,
Even if you declare free will.

Learn who you are today.
Avoid regrets and sorrow.
Those are the emotions that
Always darken tomorrow.

Wrote my own religion,
Monumental spiritual montage,
Doctrine of disappointment,
Commandments of self-sabotage

✝ Fate of Princess Perception ✝

Find God in yourself,
Issued so many evictions,
Or God will find you.
Hell is a slaughterhouse of convictions.

Conceal your boozing,
Conceal your bruising,
Falling apart while
Falling down.

Storm your own castle
That hides your sanity's nest.
Jealous of your lost throne,
Where purity once could rest.

Showers of drama,
Showers of trauma,
Slowly slipping into
Contentment's gown.

Disconnected by everyone.
Who shunned who when it began,
Sole survivor of a soul.
So many mates, now there is none.

Begging for drugs,
Begging for hugs.
False reality is the God of clowns.

Purveyor of sins introduces you
To the purveyor of death.
Smiling, waiting for you
To buy your last breath.

His heart is on his sleeve.
He didn't mean to cause her alarm.
Yes he feels heartache,
So stop punching him in the arm.

He knows when he scores instantly
Or when he hit the post.
Open your eyes; he can't see
The part of you that matters most.

Stand up straight.
Look him in the eyes.
Stop looking down.
Your life is flying by.

She's not engaged.
He's definitely not looking for a wife.
Everyone would be happier
If they were engaged in life.

The only diamonds are in her eyes.
Sorry, he doesn't have money to spend.
He can't justify that purchase anymore.
Children are starving; there's nothing to defend.

Because it means something to her,
She chooses to make it symbolic.
Wasted money is wasted time.
No need to preach to this alcoholic.

✝ Turn on the Aggression ✝

Time to turn on
The aggression.
Excuse me?
This is my profession.

Working every day
Gets rid of my depression.
Play an hour each Sunday,
MVP of this violent session.

Turn it on, turn it off
Within a split second.
So fast there's no detection.
Always striving for perfection.

I am here to carry that rock
Into the future succession.
All my Xs and Os
Are not signs of affection!

Carry on the discussions
As we risk concussions.
So worried about the rock,
Relegate us to off-season talk.

✝ Piano Woman ✝

Every note stings as keys are hit.
Within me notes resonate.
Will my songs ever be performed?
Will my lack of talent be my fate?

Our romance is written in my book.
You read too closely, you'll overlook.
Playing notes, remaining paperless,
Coping with my nothingness.

Your music is held within my heart.
Feels like your piano is on my chest.
Ticktock of the metronome
Reminds me I'm unknown.

Everything is black and white.
Paint the keys another color.
I think too much; I hesitate.
Your concerto flows as I meditate.

Subconscious wanderings,
Conversations never happening.
How can we speak to be certain?
Don't leave before the final curtain.

✝ Sustain ✝

I play hopeless.
I play despair.
All are notes
Still in the air.

I am alone,
Playing in vain.
Writing in circles
Until I see the bloodstain.

Lines that define time,
All notes played before.
Lines written and erased
Until blood stains a littered floor.

One note at a time
Drips as slow as I can count.
Music will be my last heartbeat
From this world when I dismount.

✝ Settle This ✝

How do you want to settle this?

Words or handshake?
Handshake or pen?
Pen or fist?
Fist or knife?
Knife or bullet?
Bullet or bomb?
Bomb or words?

How can we get along?

Ignore or talk?
Talk or walk?
Walk or make a stand?
Make a stand or create a border?
Create a border or build a fence?
Build a fence or build a wall?
Build a wall or talk?

Agree to disagree.

Yet you won't leave it alone.

How can we get along?

How can we settle this?

✝ **Professor Olson** ✝

This is what they should have told you
On your first day of college:
Your life is meant to be happy.
This grants you a lifetime of knowledge.

Write your own obituary.
Leave plenty of room for revisions.
Mistakes and choices, good and bad,
Collections of moments' decisions.

Follow your own vision
Of what you want your life to be.
No matter what happens,
Remember to enjoy life and be happy.

Have expectations for you, not others.
Laugh at yourself if you change your mind.
Forgive yourself when experience teaches
You a lesson to be more kind.

If a belief held deeply
Is proven false,
Take it easy on yourself.
Living is a tricky waltz.

Promises will be broken.
Lies will be told.
Smile because you expected them.
Not easy, but be bold.

You may be happy
And enjoy life
With or without a
Partner, husband, or wife.

Define your own success.
Some may be brilliant.
In order to reach your goal,
Everyone has to be resilient.

Learn to control your mind.
Have emotional intelligence.
Thoughts and feelings are not always true.
Calmness reveals their relevance.

Becoming a memory is just another event.
Everyone seems to have death aversion.
Treat my passing with a smile that we met.
My memory smiles back from its excursion.

✝ Not as Easy as 1, 2, 3 ✝

Public Life	Private Life	Secret Life
Person	Spouse	Artist
Middle	Beginning	End
Present	Past	Future
Love	Hate	Indifference
Brain	Mind	Dark Passenger
Moral	Civil	Criminal
Ego	Superego	Id
Natural	Beautiful	Ugly
Nothing	Something	Everything
Sober	Socially	Frequently
Never	Sometimes	Always
Someone	Everyone	No One
Yellow	Green	Red
Black	White	Gray
Friend	Muse	Obsession
Earthling	Alien	Extraterrestrial
Planet	Stars	Galaxy
Agnostic	Religious	Atheist
Human	Angel	God
Human	Demon	Satan
Purgatory	Heaven	Hell
Us	You	Me

✝ Dead-I-Cation ✝

You taught me to kiss
In the abyss.
Desperation of humanity.

Never thought I'd go there,
Hoping time after time
You could actually love.
Definition of insanity.

Issues you're not willing to
Address,
Your solution, getting drunk with anyone
And undress.

So cheers to you and
Whomever you are with.
Loving you and love to you
Will always be a myth.

You are incapable of love!
You are 100 percent a lie!
Count the lives you have damaged.
When will you begin to indemnify?

Thank you and goodbye, love.
It was a painful education.
This is for your "love," your
Dead-I-Cation.

† "Leeway"* †

Sick of watching
From battleships,
Always ready to destroy
Relationships.

Engines powered by hate,
Fear, lies, and unrest,
Needing love and safety,
Searching for each other's treasure chest.

In teardrops from our eyes
We saw lifetimes of pain.
Each tear carried memories
Of a past hurricane.

Can't believe we are drowning
This close to the shore.
Sandy beach inches below us,
We can't stand up anymore.

We've carried these anchors
Through stormy weather.
Weather keeps getting worse.
Only tide, not time can reverse.

Anchors forcing our last breath.
Hate to lie, scared to death to confide.
We have to let the anchors go
Because we're already dead inside.

Can't hold on any longer,
Continuing to bite our tongues.
Let go only for a chance to survive
Before black water fills our lungs.

Internal compass directs us
To a deep red sky.
It's getting late to continue.
We deserve a fighting chance to survive.

We admit our sand castles
Have washed away.
We built them as best we could.
This time not made of sand
That turns to maybe, if, and would.

Most treasures are buried in
Crumbled ships from being breached.
There we are, so cold and deep.
If we never try, we'll never be reached.

Sea serpents and mermaids,
They do exist.
It's amazing what you find
When you don't fear the heavy mist.

We know we have
Become thirsty.
Drinking saltwater
Will kill you and me.

Can't let Kraken
Touch us again.
No more chances from
His grips and grin.

To each other's shores,
Still a lot of swimming
Where we know our
Waters are forgiving.

"Leeway" single. Song can be found on all platforms. ©2020 Kirk Olson and 5050songs Inc.

✞ Nightly Death ✞

I wake to the saddest sunrise.
My bed has become a tomb.
I rise with hope thin as a cobweb,
Desperate to hear your voice,
Desperate to hold your hand.
Is our love real?
There is no floor below me.
Catch me, I am falling.

I die every night
When I close my eyes.
Everything I dream is a nightmare.
Desperate to hear your voice,
Desperate to hold your hand.
I know the dreams are not real.
There is no floor below me.
Catch me, I am falling.

You are the last woman I thought I'd kiss.
Remembering your beautiful smile,
Staring into your eyes, smelling your sweet skin.
Desperate to hear your voice,
Desperate to hold your hand.
Are we still in love?
How far will I fall?
Please catch me now!

Sun sets.
Dreadful, lonely night creeps in to remind me
My dreams won't be real.
You are not lying beside me.
I lie down about to die again,
Desperate to hear your voice,
Desperate to hold you.

✝ Dead to Me ✝

Hearing you say, "I love you so much,"
Those words never meant so little.
Your actions proved you were unbelievable,
Making the thought of us so brittle.

There's not enough time left
In your life to apologize.
Every time you said you loved me,
Each time with different lies.

You won't hear from me.
My big amour,
Stop the lies; truth is
I never knew you for sure.

I just thought it was drugs and alcohol.
I did not know people like you exist.
Mentally damaged from your youth,
I learned you became a narcissist.

But it's way too late for us.
You're still a nightmare for a few.
It's just their fate
To love the fake you.

Your life is so tragic.
Your death will be too.
There is no love
On the streets for you.

So many times
I should have left it at goodbye.
Embarrassed that I was used
As part of the chain in your supply.

Without your 100 percent devotion,
There will be no discovery
That there is no magic
On the road to recovery.

Next tear about you that I shed
Will be from inside a pew.
Crying at your funeral
Will be next time I see you.

You are unable to feel empathy.
I know you are confused
Because you are so familiar,
Using people and being used.

You're a pathological liar.
I'm a logical path to living higher.
Spiraling to your death faster
Than anybody I have ever seen prior.

I used to think that you
Were broken and hopeless.
I loved you.
You couldn't care less.

You're barely alive now.
Now you're dead to me.
I would've given you the world
Until I realized you exist to deceive.

It's really not regrettable
That you will be so forgettable.
One lie after another, this one was the best,
Claiming you will always love me, you failed that test.

So I hope you read this and weep
Enough to hate yourself from afar.
Become who you are supposed to be,
Not die as who you are.

✝ Not Supposed To ✝

Pulled me in with a smile,
Wrapped me up with a laugh,
Sealed me with a kiss.
Sacrificed me on whose behalf?

You decided you could not stay.
Kissing softly and slow,
Leaving regardless of the time.
Enjoyed my pain as you would go.

You left me so many times.
Just walked away.
Was it easier to run
Than pushing all the way?

Was it harder to push?
Much easier to pull.
All those broken pieces
Of my heart that was full.

Wondering how hard to push?
Off a cliff my life had flown.
Living in solitude,
Abandoned, you knew I was dying alone.

Time and love
Can't be frozen.
No rhyme or reason
We were chosen.

Not supposed to like you;
Definitely not supposed to love.
Everyone said to run.
You teased me with intervention from above.

Everyone began screaming at me to run.
I could not even turn around.
My love blinded me.
My heartbeat drowned out all sound.

Whispering and writing me,
Begging me to take you back.
Responded with forgiveness and hope,
Discovering soul-destroying lies that became fact.

Yes, maybe the timing
Was all wrong.
Hope you can fix your life.
Now is over; to the future we can't belong.

We did not have a prayer.
You left it all to chance.
Running from man to man,
You brought death to our romance.

✝ love Letters In A Row ✝

Lost In A dystopian life,
Constricted by booze and dope.
Living In A new world,
Where there is boundless hope.

Learned In A rush
How things can go wrong.
Let In A good man,
He'll write your song.

Love Is About the beauty
That was not inside her.
Love Is About her lies
That killed our future.

Long Is A road
To true recovery.
Life Is A trail of damage
Until self-love is a discovery.

Look In A mirror.
No one there to coddle.
Look In A dream,
Instead of a bottle.

✝ Goodnight, Sweetheart ✝

If you ever wake in the dark,
You'll know you're alone.
Only had to stretch an inch or two,
Now you won't feel me next to you.

Used to sleep with your cheek
Upon my chest.
I was once a thankful man.
Now I am reminded of your unrest.

I wrapped my arms around you.
Everything just melted away.
Every problem had to wait
While my world was given away.

I am not your hero.
I am a victim of your unfaithful lust.
Nothing left to provide shelter,
Our love died because of your distrust.

Nothing more beautiful than
Your once-trusted kiss when I was stressed.
Our presence in each other's lives
Now only hell has blessed.

✝ Sunset Kills Us ✝

I always knew the days couldn't last.
Didn't believe they'd be over so damn fast.
I closed my eyes, opened them so many times you were gone,
Left here thinking, writing my sad songs.

Sun sets, and I sit here alone.
Tide goes out with my soul I loaned.
Sea glass shatters, ripping my beliefs to shreds.
False memories are gone with any heart threads.

Everything you said was a lie, and I'm gone.
The last betrayal was your last unforgivable sin.
More shattered sea glass won't make you reappear.
You left me; you'll never get a chance to leave me again.

Tide keeps its promises, more sea glass tomorrow.
Absolutely no more of my time for you to borrow.
As this sunset kills us, and this day
I'm not a fool; you were never going to stay.